Soccer Drills

A 100 Soccer Drills, Strategies and Skills to Improve your Game

Chest Dugger

Table Of Contents

Table Of Contents 2

DISCLAIMER 4

Introduction 7

Most Important Aspects of Soccer for the Individual 10

Most Important Aspects of Soccer for the Team 17

Keeping Possession 21

Short Passing Skills 31

Shooting 39

Long Passes 47

Dribbling 56

Fitness 60

Communication 67

Team Passing 74

Team Interceptions 81

Possession 89

Final Words 96

Free Gift Included

As part of our dedication to help you succeed in your career, we have sent you a free soccer drills worksheet. This is the "Soccer Training Work Sheet" drill sheet. This is a list of drills that you can use to improve your game; as well as a methodology to track your performance on these drills on a day-to-day basis. We want to get you to the next level.

Click on the link below to get your free drills.

https://soccertrainingabiprod.gr8.com/

ABOUT THE AUTHOR

Chest Dugger is a pen name for our soccer coaching team, Abiprod. Abiprod is a team of passionate professional coaches and fans, based in UK and Australia. You can check us out at www.abiprod.com

We have been fans of the beautiful game for decades, coaching junior and senior teams. Like every soccer fan around the globe, we watch and play the beautiful game as much as we can. Whether we're fans of Manchester United, Real Madrid, Arsenal or LA Galaxy; we share a common love for the beautiful game.

Through our experiences, we've noticed that there's very little information for the common soccer fan who wants to escalate his game to the next level. Or get their kids started on the way. This is especially the case for those who live outside Europe and South America. Expensive soccer coaching and methodology is pretty rare in even rich countries like USA and Australia.

Being passionate about the game, we want to get the message across to as many people as possible. Through our soccer coaching blog, books and products; we aim to bring the best of soccer coaching to the world. Though we are starting off in USA and Australia, anyone who's passionate about the beautiful game can use our tactics and strategies.

DISCLAIMER

Copyright © 2017

All Rights Reserved

No part of this eBook can be transmitted or reproduced in any form including print, electronic, photocopying, scanning, mechanical, or recording without prior written permission from the author.

While the author has taken the utmost effort to ensure the accuracy of the written content, all readers are advised to follow information mentioned herein at their own risk. The author cannot be held responsible for any personal or commercial damage caused by information. All readers are encouraged to seek professional advice when needed.

Introduction

Whether known as football or, as in the US, soccer; the 'beautiful game' is the most popular sport in the world. The best players earn millions of dollars per year, and the greatest clubs are icons in their regions. Children love putting down a couple of jerseys and having a kick around. It is, globally, the team sport that has the greatest public participation and, at the highest level such as the World Cup, top leagues and cup finals, matches are watched live by tens of thousands of cheering fans. Support is only limited by stadium size, with tens or even hundreds of millions following their team on TV.

It is therefore no surprise that so many people love to play the game, and want to become better at it. Youngsters dream of becoming the next Pele, Messi, Maradona or Ronaldo. This book offers coaches and players an insight into how to become a better soccer player. There are chapters on the role of the individual in this team game, and the role of the team in a sport lit up by the brilliance of individuals. There are drills listed to help the player and his side. Indeed, it is drills that lead to players becoming experts, as good as they can be. Drills take the individual components of soccer and allow practice in a pressure free, or pressure controlled, environment.

Imagine that a game of soccer is like an English Literature examination. For that test, you get taught the information you need to know; you practice using that learning in tests, discussions and essays. You work on it on your own, making sure that your mind is fit enough to tackle the challenge of the final exam.

What you very much do not want is to be learning new concepts under the pressure of the examination hall. That is the place to show what you can do, not try out risky ideas.

In many ways, sport is the same. For soccer, the examination is the match; learning the skills is like gaining your understanding of Shakespeare; applying those skills is automatic in the chaos of the game. Those exercises you worked on in training ensure that you are fit enough to survive the game at your best.

And just like a piece of great literature, so a great soccer performance is made up of separate elements, which combine to produce the art form that is the 'beautiful game.' Just as you could examine character, plot, language and metaphor when studying 'Macbeth', a great performance in soccer is made up of control, passing, shooting, defending and teamwork.

Those elements can be broken down, practiced and perfected during drills. The drill allows for experimentation; failure and error does not matter. Indeed, we learn through our mistakes. There is less pressure during a drill, so time can be spent getting the individual skills and movements right. A good coach can help a player focus on areas of weakness. Pressure can be introduced slowly, and in a controlled way, ratcheted up to recreate conditions more like those in the match situation.

During practice sessions, often younger (and probably older!) players long for the 'game.' 'Can we play a match now?' is the sort of request coaches of younger players will recognize readily. And that is fine, a little match – perhaps one that reinforces the skills on which the session focuses on, makes a fun and useful end to a coaching session. But drills are crucial in helping players to become the best they can be.

These skill sessions can be focused on the individual, working on technique perhaps in groups of two to four; they can also be larger group drills, or whole team activities which help mutual understanding and coordination.

Most Important Aspects of Soccer for the Individual

There are many individual elements that go together to make the up the best players. Here we look at several of them.

One: Attitude and Commitment

Perhaps most important of all, the best players want to get better, they want to show what they can do, and they want to win. They will place the team above themselves as individuals. They will work on the parts of their game that are weakest, and seek to improve them.

They will be leaders on the pitch and in the changing room, challenging negativity and encouraging their team mates, especially younger ones, or newer members, of their squad.

These attributes will combine to mean that they get an enormous enjoyment from playing the game. Every game, every friendly, every practice session will be important to them, and from their commitment to these, they will become the very best that they can be. And during the game, the players with the best attitude and commitment are the ones who do not let their heads drop when things go against them, do not blame their team mates or the referee, but who continue to fight on, hoping to turn around a score line.

These are the kinds of players who often end up as captain. As many managers have said, the very best teams have eleven captains.

Two: Physical and Mental Attributes

These are elements in which players can only work to improve within the limits of their physiology. The physical elements needed for a footballer can be broken down into several parts.

1.*Physical fitness*: Children tend to be naturally fit; if they are enthusiastic enough to be coming to training, play in the team, then they are likely to be active in other parts of their life. Sadly, when we reach adulthood, other demands on our time can see that fitness dissipate. Regular training will help to maintain it, such as finding time to go for a thirty minute jog, or spend an hour in the gym. Along with football training and playing matches, this will help the amateur to maintain sufficient fitness for a reasonable standard of soccer.

2.*Height and strength*: There is not much that can be done regarding the first of these attributes, but training and, if the standard is high enough, some work in the weights' room of the gym will help to improve the second element. While very top players do possess strength, even those of smaller stature, it is also true that soccer is a sport that accommodates different heights, body shapes and various levels of strength. After all, Lionel Messi, generally considered the greatest player of the last five or so years, needed growth hormone treatment when he was a boy because he was so small. Even now, playing for Barcelona and Argentina, he makes up for his diminutive stature with his speed and reading of the game.

3.*Speed*: This can be worked on with sprinting practice, but as players improve they can accommodate a lack of pace with their reading of the game. In defence, dropping off a striker and ensuring that you are in the best position to intercept protects a lack of pure speed. Up front, similar tricks can be applied. The Arsenal and France striker, Olivier Giroud, is blessed with only average speed for a forward, but still scores regularly for club and country through his aerial strength, excellent footwork and ability to be in the right place at the right time.

4.*Touch:* Probably the most important technical part of a player's make up, the ability to control the ball quickly creates the opportunity to make better decisions, and use the ball under less pressure. The Dutch maestro Dennis Bergkamp was an example of a player for whom the ball appeared stuck to his feet; similarly, his older countryman Johann Cruyff appeared to own magnetic boots, so attached to them was the ball. For these two greats, playing the game was easier because the ball was always there, under their control. We have a chapter of drills coming up which will help players develop their touch.

5.*Reading of the Game*: This is quite a difficult concept to define. Perhaps it is best explained as, that quality of predicting where the ball we end up, and the runs that players – colleagues and opponents – will make. As an ability, it is partly innate, partly learned through experience, partly drilled through practice. Defensively, it allows players to pop up at the right time; offensively it lets strikers pick up rebounds and deflections, or arrive late into the box to finish off a great move. Creatively, it leads to the sort of wonder-passing which opens up a defence. The great German midfielder, Mesut Ozil, is an example of player who 'sees' the pass, and thus creates many opportunities for his team mates.

Three: The Skills to Play their Position.

Clearly, the skills of the goalkeeper are often different to the talents of the centre forward, although these days most goalkeepers at the highest level are expected to be comfortable with passing the ball, able to start attacks with a precise delivery out wide. However, even within the outfield positions, there are differences.

As a coach, it is important not to pigeon-hole young players too early. The big lad who can kick it miles might seem like an ideal centre half, but within a year, his friends might have overtaken him height wise, and he may have lost that opportunity to develop the skills of an attacking midfielder.

However, as players grow, many will tend to drift to certain playing roles. Those who can operate in a number of positions offer more to the team, but, still bearing this in mind, these are the typical skills that are often looked for in particular positions:

Goalkeeper: Some size, once playing at adult level, is important. Good athleticism and strong handling are other requirements. A goalkeeper needs to be naturally brave, and should also kick well.

Centre Half: A good reading of the game is vital, to anticipate attacking runs and passes. Some pace is an advantage; being good in the air and physically strong are often pre-requisites; an ability to bring the ball out of defence to launch an attack can turn a good stopper into a player able to offer more to the team.

Wing Backs: A growing role in modern football, and perhaps one of the hardest to master. A good wing back is strong going forward but also knows how to defend. Speed is crucial, as is a good level of overall fitness. The ability to cross well is an advantage.

Full Backs: See wing back, but with more emphasis on defence.

CDM (Central Defensive Midfielder): Many teams play with one or two of these players. A 'good engine', that is the ability to keep running, is crucial. A clear understanding of the game – when to protect the defence, when to launch forward into attack, is also very important.

Central Midfield: Skills and attributes should be similar to a CDM, but a good central midfielder will be expected to add goals to his repertoire as well. A good shot, two footedness and an ability to arrive late in the box to pounce on a loose ball are all vital qualities.

Wide Midfield/Wing: Pace is needed here, the ability to knock the ball past the defender and beat them with speed. Also, the ability to cross well – after all, there is little point getting into a strong position then not being able to deliver a good ball. Wingers are expected to score goals.

Number 10: Today, often where the most creative footballers play. Two good feet, an eye for a pass (and the ability to deliver it), combined with regular goal scoring are the expectations for such a player. Good dribbling skills can add an extra dimension, causing uncertainty in defenders' minds.

Centre Forward: Two distinct kinds of player remain in this position. There is the strong, powerful player who is good with his or her back to goal, can bring in team mates with clever short passes and who is strong in the air. Perhaps more so, today, centre forwards are skilful, two footed players with a burst of speed and coolness in front of goal. Whichever type of player you are, as a centre forward you are expected to score goals.

Most Important Aspects of Soccer for the Team

The definition of what makes a great soccer team could lead to endless arguments. It is the topic of conversation in many a bar. If we briefly look at some of the greats, in terms of teams, then it is clear that a number of factors emerge to help us identify the characteristics of the best teams.

Tactical Brilliance:

The great Dutch teams of the 1970s – they reached two consecutive World Cup finals, both of which they should have won; the Spanish national side of the 2010s, and the Barcelona team of that era – each of these sides played in a way that others could not counter. The Dutch, of course, invented total football, where every player was capable of performing every role. Whoever was there did the required job. The Spanish sides and their tika-taka play moved the ball so quickly that their opponents could not get near it. That these teams benefitted from the likes of Cruyff, Messi and Iniesta certainly added a further advantage.

Amazing Front Line:

Some teams have been so strong up front that they have simply outscored the opposition. The Mighty Magyars of Hungary, who would surely have won the world cup had not their great player, Ferenc Puskas, been 'assassinated' by a German defender in an earlier round; the amazing Real Madrid of the 1960s (also featuring Puskas, alongside Di Stefano) the Brazilians of 1970, Pele and Jairzinho to the fore. However, although strong going forward, these teams were no weaklings defensively, and that the opposition hardly touched the ball was also a factor in their success.

Great All-Round Sides:

The English Premier League is unique in major competitions in that every team is capable of beating any other. Because of the enormous amounts of television money in the English Premier League, even teams who eventually end up relegated regularly defeat sides in the top six. This is untrue of Germany, Italy (to a lesser extent) and Spain, where there are perhaps two or three strong contenders, and maybe three or so others who spring the odd surprise; for the remainder, they simply do not compete with the best. The Arsenal 'Invincibles' team of 2004, undefeated throughout the campaign, was built from strength in all positions. The speed of Thierry Henry, the guile of Dennis Bergkamp, the power of Gilberto Silva and Patrick Viera and the defensive quality of Sol Campbell and Ashley Cole.

Therefore, we can see that all the best teams were strong throughout the side, although they may have been better in certain departments. They kept possession well, and had players of particular brilliance.

For most of us, of course, as coaches and players, we will not ascend anywhere close to the levels listed above. But we still look to develop our play to the highest level it can be. But although we will not have the pleasure of working with players of such technical ability, there are other factors which are possessed by all great sides, and on which we can certainly work with our own players.

They are:

Communication

Attitude

Flexibility

(Plus the best skill level the group can achieve.)

Communication is crucial; sport is by its nature competitive, soccer adds to this competitiveness physical challenge and speed. Communication adds another aspect to a player's ability to read the game, to know whether they have time on the ball, or whether to lay it off quickly. It helps them to know what their team mates are doing.

Attitude, as we saw with individual characteristics, is crucial. There needs to be a team mind set to compete as hard as possible, to keep heads up when things go against you, to keep playing until the end. Many games that have seemed lost have changed in the last ten minutes, sometimes even in injury time itself.

Finally, *flexibility*. Playing soccer is not just about what you do as a team, but also how the opposition play. That ability to adapt formation, close down more quickly or look to play on the break marks out the most successful sides from the also rans.

Keeping Possession

General Information on Diagrams

Most of the drills described over the next chapters include a simple explanatory diagram. For these, the dots (and occasionally squares) represent players and the lines refer to the movement of the ball (white) and movement of players (grey/blue). Sometimes, a square is used to show the need for grid (painted, or made of cones) and lines are added to divide up areas of the pitch.

Possession

Control of the ball is the fundamental skill without which no player can be an effective part of their team. Indeed, at the highest levels, the first thing at which a scout will look is their subject's ball control, often referred to as their 'first touch'. The best examples of this will demonstrate the following:

- Keeping the ball close to the body, adapting to the proximity of the nearest opponent.

- Positioning the ball so that it can be laid off to an opponent easily
- Using the body to protect the ball from an opponent's tackle

When coaching there are certain key points to emphasise to your students:

- Get your body in line with the passage of the ball as quickly as possible
- Whichever part of the body you are going to use to control the ball should relax slightly on impact, cushioning the ball, but preventing from becoming stuck under, for example, the foot
- Make sure that as much as your body as possible is behind the ball as you control it.

An individual practice not displayed below is to juggle the ball. This helps to develop dexterity, and can be either as a solo activity, or group challenge. For example, younger players love to be challenged to juggle the ball ten times without it touching the ground, while six players can try to work as a team to keep the ball off the floor for ten touches.

Practice Drills

Drill One: Square Pass

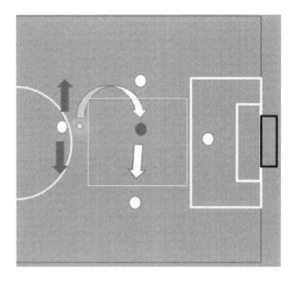

Using grids (these can be marked out with cones laid, for example, eight metres apart, or can be ready painted onto a pitch):

- Position a player (shown below in white) on each side of the grid. These players can move laterally along their line of the grid and up to one metre behind it.
- A fifth player (blue/grey) is in the middle of the grid.
- A white player passes the ball to blue/grey.
- Blue/Grey must control the ball, and pass the ball to any of the four whites.
- The control and pass it back to blue/grey.

- After a couple of minutes, the players rotate.

Emphasise the three key skills bullet pointed above.

Development

- Start the drill with a throw from white, to help practice control with different parts of the body. With more able players, the grid can be extended, and lofted passes introduced to challenge grey even more. However, here grey should still be encouraged to return the pass on the ground.
- Set a number of touches for the grey player; for example, start with three, reduce to two, and then one.
- Encourage the whites to be on the move along their lines. This develops communication and also helps with passing as well as encouraging grey to get his/her body position right as early as possible

Drill Two: Square Pass with opponents

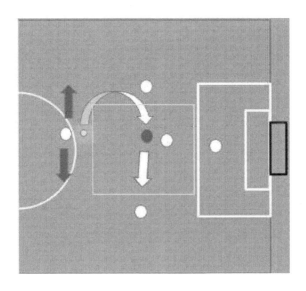

The drill is the same as above, but a sixth player is added. This player is inside the grid with grey, and aims to pressure the ball.

Initially, start with just a presence, then allow the player to jockey to help blue/grey develop balance and ensure his body is protecting the ball. Finally, allow the opponent to try to win the ball.

Although it seems similar, this is a much more challenging drill.

Drill Three: Using the whole body

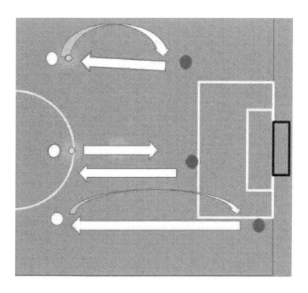

- The top white player is throwing the ball for control using the chest, thigh and raised foot.
- The middle white player is driving passes firmly along the floor, using their laces is a good enough player.
- The bottom white player is lofting and chipping long passes. If you are working with younger players who struggle to do this, they can throw the ball.
- The blue/grey players are working on controlling the ball, and returning it with a sharp pass to their white player.
- In each case, the grey players must employ the skills mentioned earlier to control the ball successfully.
- In the first example, when chesting the ball, players should make their chest as big a possible, before relaxing it slightly at the last

minute to keep the ball close to them. Using the arms for balance is very important with control

- While controlling the driven pass, players need to watch the path of the ball carefully, tracking it and getting their body in line, since the ball could bounce, and accuracy is likely to be lost from the passer.

- In the third example, where the pass has been lifted, the grey player needs to develop the ability to make decisions, learning which part of their body works best for them, if their feet are ruled out of the equation.

Development

Increasing distance can add extra challenge, plus the drill can be developed to emphasise practice on the weakest part of their control. Pressure can be increased by whites having a supply of balls, and firing off the next delivery as soon as the previous one has been dealt with.

Drill Four - Whole Body Under Pressure

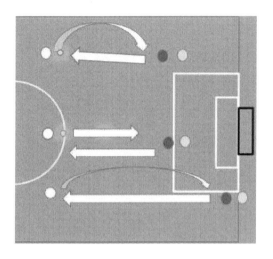

Once again, we add to the straightforward drill by adding an opponent. This is especially useful as it adds the dimension of decision making to the grey player. He must judge how far he can move to the ball, and which part of the body to use for control while ensuring that he prevents his opponent from intercepting the ball or getting in a tackle before the ball can be laid off.

Drill Five – Segments

This is a brilliant drill which develops many aspects of an individual's game. It brings in communications, decision making, passing and interception. It works superbly with group training as well as team work is crucial in playing it successfully. Segments is a great way to finish any session of drills. It can be played with four, five or six players in each 'team'.

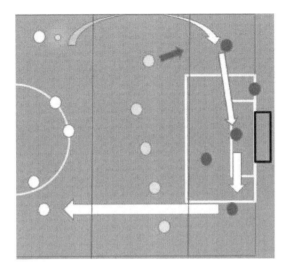

- Half a pitch is divided into three equal segments as below.
- The aim is to get the ball from segment one (white) to segment 3 (blue/grey) without the yellow/pale greys in segment two interception.
- The ball must then be passed back from segment three to segment one.
- If the ball is intercepted or goes out of play, then the team at fault swap with the 'defensive' team occupying segment 2.
- One player only from segment two is allowed to pressure ball when it is in segment one or segment three.

- Control of the initial ball is essential, as when the drill works well, the defensive team apply rapid pressure.
- From there, it is up to the team to create the time and space to play a pass-through segment two to the other end of the pitch.

Development

- Allow the pressuring players to swap, so the comes back and another, better placed player, is allowed to challenge as the team attempt to create space for the pass
- Allow a second player to pressure the ball.
- Shrink the playing area
- Impose restrictions to develop the skill being practiced, e.g. if the drill is to work on chest control, only allow lofted passes.

Short Passing Skills

For best accuracy, short passing should be played with the instep. A great tip for coaches and players is to always practice passing using both feet, so working on the left foot, then the right.

Key Points

- Approach the ball from an angle of about 30 degrees.
- Get your non-kicking foot close to the ball.
- Make sure that your weight is planted forwards, with your head over the ball. This way, the pass will stay on the ground, which makes control for your team mate easier.
- Get to know your team mates, so that you can pass to their favoured foot (if they have one).

Drill One: Simple Grid Passing

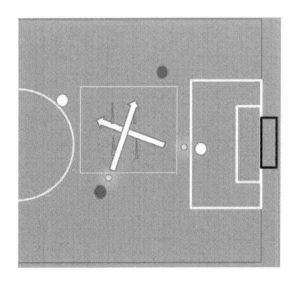

- Use the grid with a smaller square in the middle.
- Two players (grey, below) pass across the grid, making sure that the ball goes through the middle square
- Once this is mastered, two more players practice across the grid (yellow/pale grey, below). This means that timing of the pass becomes important, to stop the balls hitting each other.
- To make the drill realistic, the players should always be on the move.

Drill Two: Passing Square

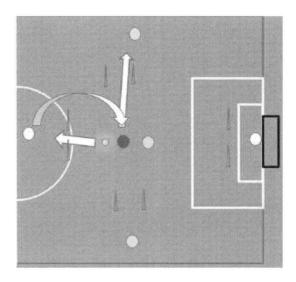

This drill is good for getting player to vary their passing.

- Mark out a rough square with four sets of two cones. The drill is for the blue/grey player in the centre.
- This player must pass the ball through the cones to a team mate, but in a different way for each.
- In this example, the two white players will receive a straight forward pass to feet, one player passed to with his left foot, the other with his right.
- The yellow/pale grey players can be one a pass to run on to, the other a lifted pass.
- The support players simply return the ball to the grey player after they have received their pass.

- Rotate periodically.

Development

- Receiving players call out the type of pass they want.
- Pressure is added to the central player with the ball played to him in a variety of ways.
- The addition of an opponent to add further pressure helps to recreate the match situation.

Drill Three: One In, One Out

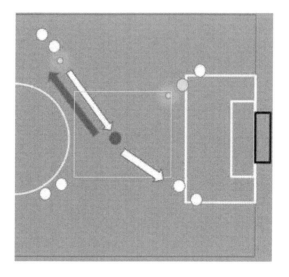

- This uses a grid, it can be made larger for less skilled players, to give more time on the ball.
- A player from one corner (white) plays the ball into the central player (grey/blue). He jogs after the ball into the centre.
- The central player turns 180 degrees with the ball and passes to corner he is now facing. He follows the ball to that corner.
- The player from the next corner (yellow/pale grey) plays the ball in for the skill to be repeated.
- The play continues.

This is a very effective warm up drill as well as good for passing, as it can start gently with pace increased as the players loosen up.

Drill Four: Pass, Pass, Shoot

This is a good drill for keeping players motivated, as everybody loves to shoot. Stress the importance of keeping the ball on the ground for this drill, until the shot stage.

(Remember to coach your players to shoot low across the body of the keeper – this is both the hardest position for the keeper to reach, and also creates the opportunity for rebounds if the shot is partially saved.)

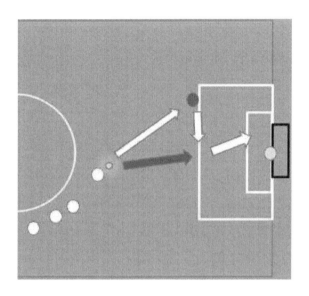

- White player passes to blue/grey and runs on (blue/grey arrow) for the return.
- Blue/Grey player passes with a simple one-two.
- White player ends with a shot.

Development

Start with two touches, then move on to one touch play.

Drill Five: Obstacle Course

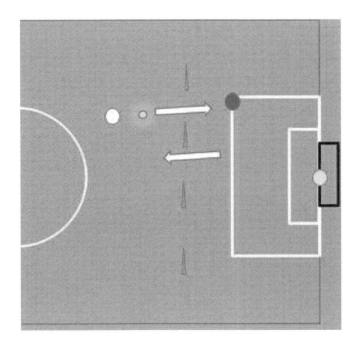

This is a good, fast action drill, also great for a warm up. The drill can be made simpler or more difficult by placing the cones further apart or closer together.

- White player passes through the cones to grey.
- Grey controls, changes the angle, and passes back between two different cones.

Development

The drill can be developed by the addition of a defender running parallel with the cones, who aims to intercept the passes. In this case, the other players must work together to make angles which allow passes to bypass the defender.

Shooting

Key points (for developing this skill) are as follows:

- Shoot through the ball, striking with the laces for extra power.
- Keep the head forward and over the ball to ensure that the shot keeps low.
- Practice with both feet; the best strikers score with either foot.
- Aim to shoot across the goal, aiming towards the far post.

Drill One – Rapid Fire

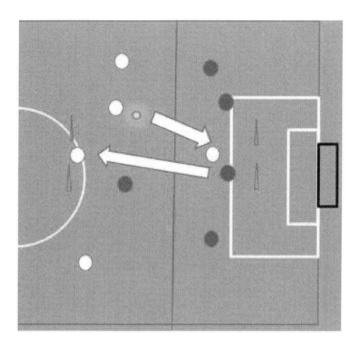

This fast action shooting drill requires a lot of balls. It is very popular, but needs careful watching as balls fly quickly.

- Set up a mini pitch with two goals approximately 30m apart. Make sure that there are two clear halves to the pitch.
- Place ten balls behind each goal.
- Each time they set up with their team in their half. One player from each side is allowed in the opponent's half. That player is there for rebounds and deflections. He or she can also pressure the passing of their opponents.

- Whites start. They must shoot from their own half. They have ten seconds maximum to get their shot away.
- Immediately the shot is away, the grey/blues get their first ball ready, and repeat.
- This continues with alternate attempts.
- The aim is to shoot quickly from your own half.

Drill Two: Pass and Shoot

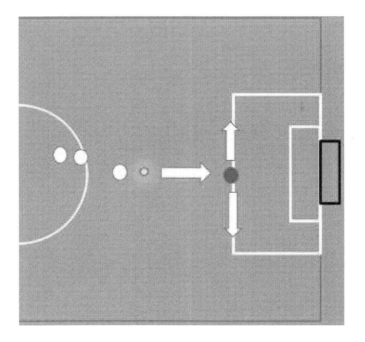

A simple but effective drill. Really encourage the player to shoot across the goal, aiming for the far post. The drill can be used with a support player chasing in the shot, looking for the rebound.

- White player passes into the feet of the blue/grey player, and sets off on run in the direction of one of the arrows, indicating with a call, or point of the arm, where he or she wants the return pass.
- The blue/grey player lays off a short pass.
- The white runs on and shoots.
- One touch can be allowed, and this can be developed by aiming for first time shooting.
- Make sure that players practice using both feet.

Drill Three: First Time Finish

Players love this drill. As coach, be aware of risk to the goalkeeper, if you use one.

Focus on the following skills.

- Striker must change the angle of his run to create space.
- Finish must be first time
- Cross needs to be pulled back, taking the keeper out of play.

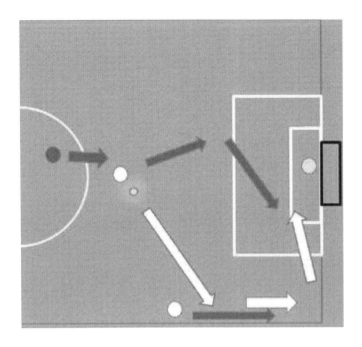

- White player passes to his colleague on the wing
- White runs to far post, then cuts at speed to the near post anticipating the cross.
- Meanwhile the white winger dribbles down the wing and pulls the ball back along the ground to the near post.
- White striker finishes first time.

Development

A defender can be added to test the striker's run. The defender should play with restraint as he knows the run the attacker will make. He is there to add pressure, not win the ball.

Drill Four: Turn and Shoot

This drill utilises the striker's first touch to create space for the shot. Shooting on the turn is more difficult than when running on to the ball, but players must still aim to keep their weight forward, their head over the ball and to strike with the laces to generate power.

The use of the defender (blue/grey player) is optional. Depending on the skill level of the players, the player can be passive or fully aiming to stop the shot.

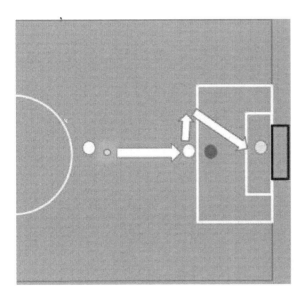

- White player feeds the ball into his striker.
- The striker controls, swivels at speed, creating a little bit of space, and shoots first time.

Drill Five: Volleys

This drill can be adapted by the feeder (grey, below) taking up different positions. For accuracy, it is best for the feeder to throw the ball rather than cross it with her feet.

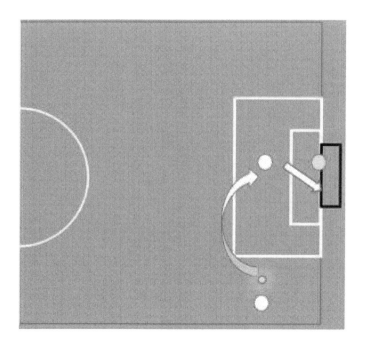

- Striker (white) points their opposite shoulder to their striking foot towards the ball, swivelling their hips.
- The body unlocks like a corkscrew, the shooting foot coming around, and the arms out for balance.
- The pace on the ball means that it is not necessary to shoot hard. Indeed, the instep can be used if the ball is at a particularly challenging height.
- The aim is to hit the target, pace will naturally be generated.

Long Passes

Fortunately, most purists would say, coaches have recognised that keeping possession is the key to success on the pitch. It preserves energy, while tiring out the opposition as they have to change position to deal with differing angles of attack. Passing on the ground is also more pleasing on the eye. For example, under the legendary Charles Hughes, the FA's former technical director in the England, the theory was to get the ball forward as quickly as possible. As England's results demonstrated, it was not the best tactic, marking one of England's less successful spells internationally.

However, the long pass does have its place. Tactically, it can turn defences, allowing speedy strikers to get in behind. Played to a skilled target man, capable of holding the ball up, it can relieve pressure and allow a quick break. Played crossfield, it can change the direction of attack quickly, causing opponents to reshape their defensive formation.

Key Coaching Points

- The pass will often have to be lifted
- Strike with the laces, leaning back slightly to achieve height (if there is plenty of space, keeping your head over the ball will stop it from rising).

- Kick slightly under the ball, also to help with lift.
- Approach from around 30 degrees
- Plant the non-kicking foot firmly beside the ball.
- Keep your eyes on the ball.
- Have a follow through with the kicking foot; this will generate distance.

Drill One: Short Pass/Long Pass

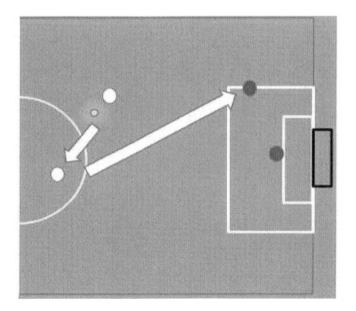

- White player hits a short pass to white
- White strikes a long diagonal pass to the blue/gray

- The drill is repeated

Development

The addition of a defender can add challenge to the exercise.

Drill Two: Long Pass and Control

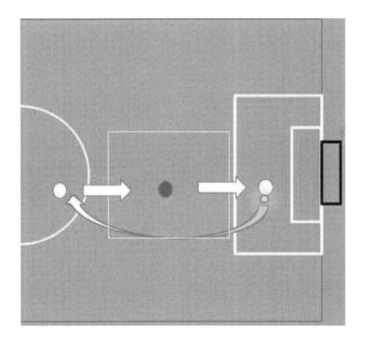

A key problem with the long pass to a team mate is that it is harder to control. This drill covers both ends of the delivery.

Depending on speed and ability, the two end players need to be around 20-25 metres apart.

- Ball is played long by the first white, over the blue/grey player in the grid (or between the cones).
- Second white gets in position to receive the ball, as per the 'control' drills earlier.
- He chooses whether to lay off first time to the grey player (via head, chest or foot) or whether to control the ball and lay it off to grey.
- Grey passes to the first white player.
- Rotate periodically.

Drill Three: Into Space

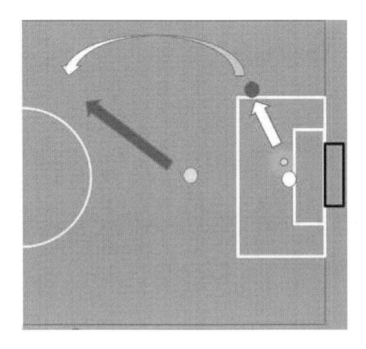

A useful drill for getting the ball away from defence to launch an attacking opportunity. This drill can be used in other parts of the pitch, and also as a cross-field pass.

- White plays a short square pass to blue/grey.
- Blue/Grey hits a long ball down the line into space.
- Meanwhile, yellow/pale grey has anticipated a set of on an angled run. He should set off as white begins his pass.

Drill Four: Backspin

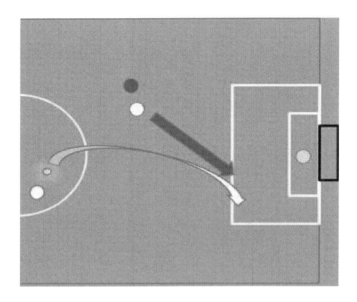

A difficult pass to play, but a good weapon to hold in the armoury. It can be played over a defender, then hold up as it bounces, giving a quick striker a chance to get behind the defence before the ball can be collected by another defender or keeper, or goes out of play. The pass tends to be lofted and can lack pace, allowing defenders to cut it out if they position in time.

Key Skills

- Lean back slightly when passing to give height.
- Strike with the toe
- Not too much follow through

- Hit the ball quite centrally

The Drill:

- White floats the pass
- His team mate and blue/grey move towards the ball
- The keeper makes a decision as to whether he can collect the ball.

It is best to limit the movement of the defensive players so that the passer develops confidence with this tricky skill.

Drill Five; Outside of the boot

Using the outside of the boot will induce curve on the ball.

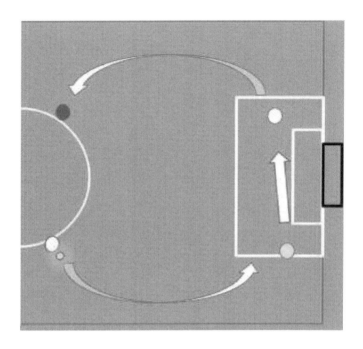

Diagram shows ball hit with outside of left foot

Key Skills:

- Hit the ball firmly with the side of the laces.
- Aim slightly wider than where you want the pass to end up – the ball will curl back.

The Drill:

- White strikes the ball with the outside of her foot, curving it to yellow/pale grey.
- Yellow/pale grey plays a short pass to white.
- White repeats long pass to grey.
- And so on, rotating as necessary.

Note, if the ball is hit with the right foot, it will curve the opposite way.

This drill can be adapted to work with a curve pass with the instep. Here, the ball will curve less dramatically. The ball should be struck with front instep, firmly, leaning back and kicking with a sweeping motion under the South East of the ball as you face it.

Dribbling

Is there anything more thrilling than watch a player beat his opponent with a moment of divine skill, or to see a striker bearing down on goal, ball under perfect control?

The drills below are very simple to set up. They require just cones to dribble around; the wider they are spaced; the faster player can travel.

The key skill when dribbling is to move the ball with the laces, so that stride pattern is not interrupted. The closer an opponent, the tighter the ball must be to the boots.

It is handy to use lines, such as grid lines or touch lines, to help players run in a straight line.

Drill One – Simple close dribbling

- Set the cones an appropriate distance apart, perhaps 1-2 metres.
- Player dribbles through the cones.
- Either, pass on to a player to dribble back, or turn and pass back to another player.

- Work on both feet.

Drill Two – Stepover

This manoeuvre creates space for a pass or to trick a defender allowing the player to dribble past.

- Create a space in the cones to allow room for the step over
- Player drops shoulder on side (e.g., right) where stepover will occur.
- Player steps (e.g., with right leg) over ball from inside to out.
- With other foot (e.g. left), player shifts the ball to the left and accelerates away.

Drill Three – Cruyff Turn

The trick, made famous by the Dutch master of the 1970s, allows a complete change of direction in play.

- Dribble through cones.
- At line, step over ball, then drag it back through your legs with the toe of the foot that completed the step over.
- Dribble back.

Drill Four – Dribbling at the keeper

This drill give practice of 1-1 against the keeper. The drill can be developed by the introduction of a defender, who starts behind the striker. To make the drill appropriate for developing dribbling skills, the defender should start far enough behind the striker to ensure that he can only catch the striker if the striker miscontrols the ball.

- Dribble directly at the keeper, pushing the ball forwards with the laces to cover the ground quickly.
  - As the keeper approaches either:
    - Shoot low, close to the body OR
    - Wait until the keeper dives at your feet and chip the ball over him.
    - Dribble the ball past, using a skill such as a turn or stepover, and shoot into the empty net.

Drill Five – Running with the ball

For this drill, either space cones widely apart, at least 8-10m, or practice without cones.

Since in a match, this skill would be employed only when there is a lot of space in front of the player, for the drill to be realistic, it should be as simple as possible.

- Ensure that the players use their laces to propel the ball forward.
- They need to ensure that their stride pattern is not broken when propelling the ball.
- Work across a pitch, or from half way to the touchline. Dribble, then a partner dribbles back.

Fitness

Fitness drills are best combined with football drills, any play with the ball is beneficial. These drills all feature the ball to some extent.

Drill One: Soccer Pursuit

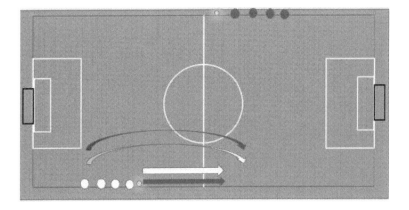

- Players line up on a touchline about 2 metres apart.
- The front player has a ball.
- The players jog continuously making their way around the pitch, while doing the following:
- The lead player dribbles for 5 metres, then steps over the ball for the team mate behind to dribble for the same distance. He too then steps over the ball.

- This continues until the ball reaches the player at the back. He next dribbles around his team mates until he reaches the front of the line, where the drill is repeated.

- A degree of competition can be added by having another team starting opposite, with the winning side being the first to catch the rear most player of the other side. Rather like a Pursuit race in cycling.

Drill Two: Tough for Defenders

A really hard drill which will help to develop physical and mental fitness.

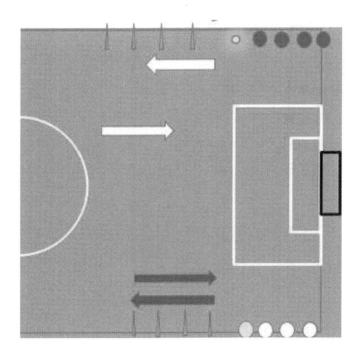

- Two teams line up as per the diagram. The whites are attacking and have a ball.
- The goalkeeper (yellow/pale grey) is leading the defence (white) line.
- On the whistle the attackers dribble through the posts then organise themselves.
- Each player must touch the ball then the dribbler must end with a shot.
- Meanwhile the defenders must go up then back down the posts, before organising themselves defensively.

- A good attack should score before the keeper is in position and set.
- Teams then swap roles.

Drill Three: Circuit

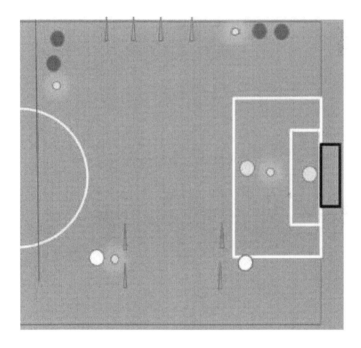

Complete the circuit with two minutes of sport, then thirty seconds of recovery, rotating through the drills.

Drills could include:

- Dribbling through posts, non-stop.
- Diving practice – player feeds the ball side to side. Keeper dives, catches and returns. Swap after one minutes.
- Individual 'keep uppy' work.
- Non-stop one touch passing.
- Running with the ball, controlling with laces. Run the width of the pitch, Cruyff turn, then repeat.

Drill Four: Distant Dribbling

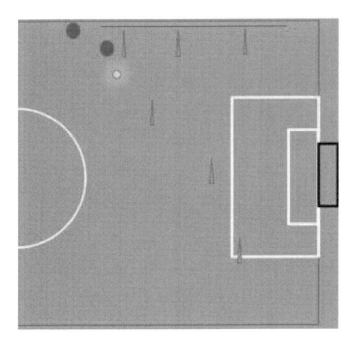

Player dribbles to the cone, turns, dribbles back to next cone, turn, dribbles once more. All to be done at speed.

Drill Five: Non-Stop

Work this drill for three minutes, then rest, then repeat. Rotate positions after each rest.

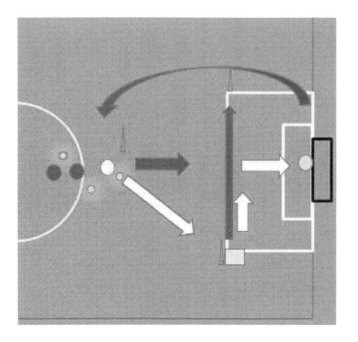

- The first player (white) passes and moves.
- He gets the return pass and shoots, or dribbles at the keeper, then collects his ball and runs to the start position.

- Player two (square) returns the pass then returns to the opposite side of the pitch ready for the next delivery.
- Players three and four (dark grey/blue) works the same as player one.
- Work out the distances so that the movement is continuous for all. Even the goalkeeper will be facing constant shots or dribbles. At any one point, the goalkeeper will be recovering her position, player one, returning with their ball, player two crossing the pitch, player three passing and running and player four getting back to position.

Communication

A team of great individuals will not often defeat a team of lesser players who combine effectively. Therefore, communication is key. The drills that follow will encourage players to communicate on the pitch, so that it becomes second nature.

Drill One: Simple Circle

This is a very simple drill, ideal for young players, or for a new group.

- Simply arrange the team in a large circle.
- One ball is used, but the drill is then made more complicated by the addition of a second and then third ball.
- Players call for the ball with 'To John, here.'
- Passers identify their target with 'John'

Drill Two: Talking Circle

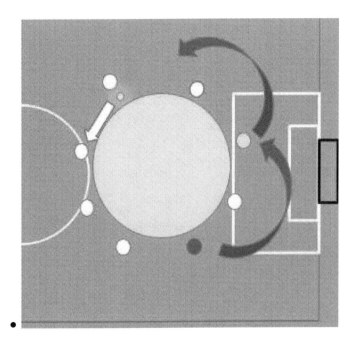

This is quite a complex drill and it is important that the coach understands it, so that the idea can be explained to players. It is, however, an excellent way to get your team working together.

- The players form into a large circle, around 15m in diameter. At least eight are needed to make the drill work.
- The players are numbered consecutively.
- Two balls are used; these start with any two players.
- The balls are passed. Number one passes to number two and so forth.

- The coach calls two numbers. For example, four and seven. These are shown by the yellow/pale grey and blue/grey circles above.
- Number four sprints to number seven's slot, and number seven to number four's space.
- The balls are passed continuously, only stopping if the target is one of the players involved in the sprint.
- As soon as the two runners are in position, two more numbers are called.
- Quite quickly, the numbers will be mixed up in the circle, and the team will need to communicate to know where each pass should be headed.

Drill Three: Prove the Point

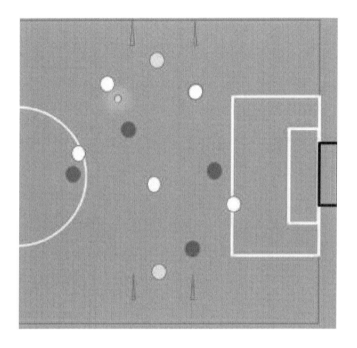

This drill works by demonstrating the importance of communication by taking it away. It is a drill that should only be used once or twice with a particular set of players.

- Set up a small sided pitch
- Play a normal game but ban any talking. Any words result in a free kick to the opposition.
- Play for a short time only, then review together the impact of no talking.

Drill Four: Spare Man

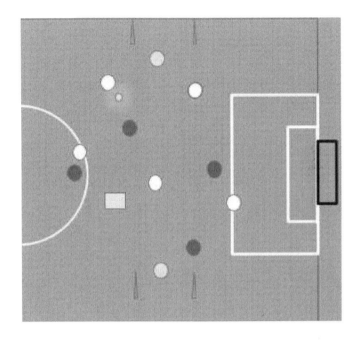

For this drill, a game is played with one spare player, shown in square symbol above. This player plays for whichever side is in possession of the ball. After a time, this can be changed to the player always being on the side of whichever team does not have possession.

The game is simple. Just a normal match but the extra player can only move and participate when given instruction, such as 'down the line' 'man on' and such like.

This drill can be developed by having a second or even a third spare player. This can really make a quick difference to a team if the players can be utilised effectively.

Drill Five: Man Management

Not a drill as such, man management is nevertheless a key skill a coach must possess to get the most out of his players, and to develop them as far as they can go.

Since we are talking about communication in this section, the coach should recognise that whilst some of his or her team are natural leaders on the pitch, directing, advising and instructing, others are more reticent. It is important to establish why. This could be just a natural shyness, or perhaps a sense of inferiority. It could be as simple as that the player is concentrating hard on the game, and does this quietly rather than with lots of chat.

Good man management identifies the reasons for lack of communication, and then helps to eradicate it. This is an individual matter, working with players one to one to ensure that they communicate. Tricks can include simple explanations of why communication is important, to creating artificial situations, such as allowing only one or two players on a team to talk.

Team Passing

Earlier in the book we looked at individual passing drills. Now we can use those skills to create more realistic match type situations. Remember, also, the 'Segments', drill, which is an excellent team passing activity.

Drill One: Squares

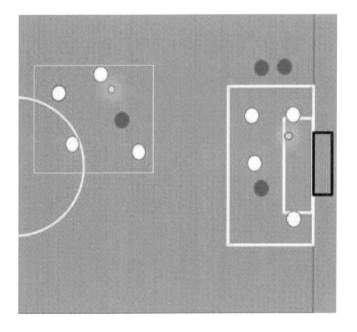

This simple drill is active and demonstrates the effectiveness of crisp passing and sharp movement.

- Create a large grid, about the size of a penalty area.
- Start with 4 v 1, but make the challenge increasingly difficult by adding in an extra defender, 4 v 2, then 4 v 3.
- The aim is to pass and move to keep the ball away from the opposition. If a pass is intercepted, then the passes becomes a defender, and the defender who made the interception joins the attacking group.

Drill Two: Pass and Shoot

Another simple to organise drill. This uses passing to create a shooting opportunity for a team.

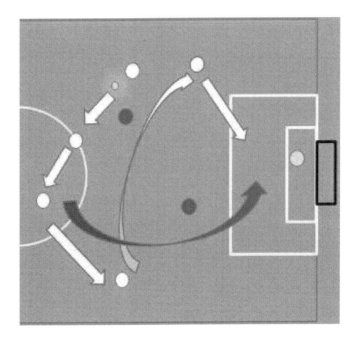

- Set up a 5 v 3 (one being a goalkeeper) drill.
- The whites must make at least four passes, then pass into the box for their team mate to shoot.
- Greys try to defend. They are not allowed in the penalty box.

Drill Three: Triangles

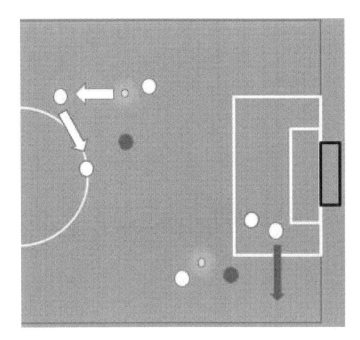

Passing triangles are a key way to create space and retain possession. Remember, in the diagram, the white lines represent the direction of the ball, and the blue/grey lines the direction of the players' movements.

- This drill uses 6 v 2, sub divided into two lots of 3 v 1.
- The drill is easy. Each group of three move to create a triangle, thus always giving a simple pass around the one opponent.
- Passes should happen within the triangle, and between triangles.
- The drill can be developed with the addition of a goalkeeper and a challenge to create space for a shot.

Drill Four: Two Touch Game

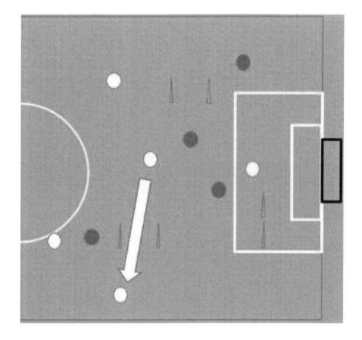

A great drill to get players thinking as well as working on their passing.

- Set up three or four pairs to goals randomly on the pitch to represent goals.
- Allow two touch passing.
- Goals as scored by passing the ball through a goal, in any direction, to a team mate.
- Make the drill harder still by introducing one touch passing.

Drill Five: Complex Team Move

Remember, the darker lines show movement of players, the lighter ones movement of the ball.

This is a complex drill, but one from which other team passing moves can be developed.

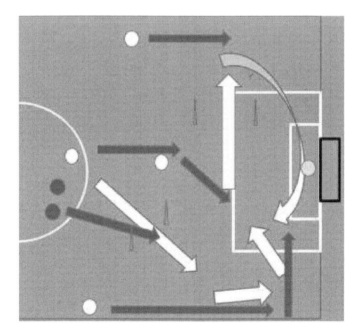

The aim is to switch play to create space for a cross or pass into the box.

- The centre circle contains three players. Two defenders (dark) and one attacker who has the ball. There is also a keeper, and three other attacking players, wide right, central and wide left. We will look at the roles of each attacking player in turn.
- Passer lays the ball wide right through the cones. He then advances to the edge of the box. His next job will be to pass the ball wide left when he receives it, then to get into the box for the cross.
- Wide right winger dribbles, pulls the ball back to the edge of the box then waits for the cross on the far post.
- Central attacker will move to the right-hand edge of the box, ready for his winger's pull back. He will then feed the ball, first time square to the original passer, who will by then be in position.
- Wide left attacker edges forward, picks up the ball that is played to him and hits a first time or second touch cross or pass into the box.
- When it works well, timing is good, and the defenders are too stretched to stop the attack. A goal often results.

Team Interceptions

The modern game sees good coaching and fit players able to defend very effectively when in formation. This means intercepting passes can often be the most effective way to launch an attack, since the defence will be out of position, having just been in attack themselves.

This phase of the game is called transition, and top coaches see it as the most important, and difficult, aspect of modern soccer. A team that can intercept, then launch an attack from that position is often one that will eventually win the game.

Interceptions usually come about from a misplaced pass, and that misplaced pass will result from pressure on the ball leading to those in possession hitting increasingly inaccurate passes.

Drill One: Applying Pressure

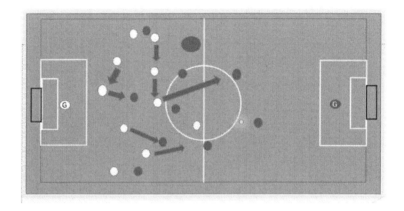

The defensive formation above is strong. The White team has a bank of four, plus a sweeper, with another bank of four in front of them. A lone striker is pressuring the defence. The arrows show movement of players. Note, the closest player pressures the ball. By working as a team, the whites will create the situation where the only two passes are back to the keeper, which is acceptable defensively, or first or second pass to the wide right midfields (blown up larger in the diagram). Firstly, that pass will have been made under pressure, so there is a risk of it being misplaced; secondly, if successful, the ball is not in a dangerous position.

The key coaching points to drill into your defence are the following:

Every player must be:

- Pressuring the ball, or
- Covering a player, or
- Covering a space.

Drill:

- Have lots of balls
- Get the attackers to set up a realistic position
- Allow the defence to organise two banks of four, or one of five and one of four
- Play the sequence
- Stress the importance of moving as a team
- As soon as possession is lost, a new sequence begins.

Drill Two: Intercepting

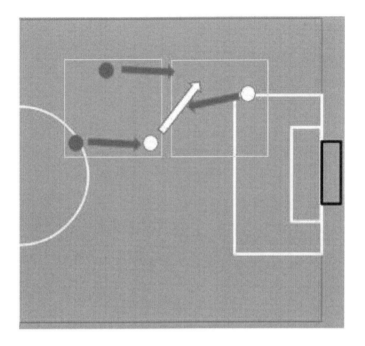

A lot of time needs to be spent allowing players to practice intercepting the pass. If their timing is out, they are temporarily lost from the defence, and space has been created for the attacking player, so judgement is crucial.

The simple drill above helps players to judge whether they can make the interception.

- Use two grids as above.

- The most defensive white will decide whether they can intercept the cross-field ball played by the darker player driving forward.

- Indicators will be whether the dark player has good control, whether his or her pass looks controlled and so on.

- The deep defensive white makes the decision whether to intercept or simply jockey the dark receiver.

- Rotate positions.

Drill Three: Small Sided Game

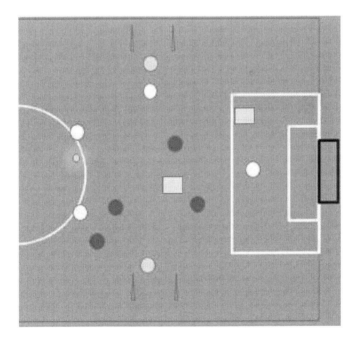

Here, the smaller sides allow for more touches of the ball. Transition is also less frequent, so play can develop more fully.

- Five v Five with two spare players (square) who represent the team in possession. (At other times, they can represent the team in defence).
- Play the game, stopping to highlight effective transition movements from both teams.

Drill Four: Transition Unopposed

This should be a short drill as it is unrealistic for the match situation.

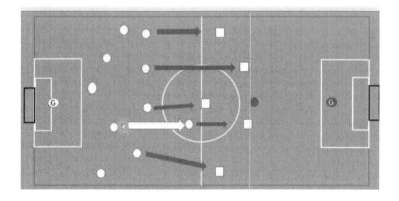

- Firstly, transition to attack.

- Set up a defensive formation.
- The coach, or one opposing player, misplaces a pass.
- The interception is made, and the team move quickly into an attacking formation.
- The 'opposition' player creates a retreating offside line where this rule is played.
- Secondly, transition to defence.
- Set up an attacking play.
- Misplace a pass to the only opponent.
- Move quickly into a defensive formation.
- Allow a time for this, for example, three seconds.
- Play stops and positions are analysed.
- In either transition phase, it is essential that all players know their roles, remembering that transition to attack can break down, and then the transition to defence is again necessary. Where teams send too many players forward at transition, this is known as 'over committing'.
- In the diagram above, the centre half intercepts and feeds in to the centre forwards. Four runners break forward, the number nine passes into one of the attackers and then also supports. The remaining outfield players move up, but keep their shape in case the attack breaks down.

Drill Five: Match Play

This is the most realistic form of drill. Play a normal game, but each time the ball is lost the coach examines the actions of team mates. If their movement is not right, the game is stopped, and the coaching point made.

Possession

Keeping possession involves using the passing and control skills we have explored earlier in the book. It means creating triangles so that there is always a simple pass on for the person in possession. It means the keeper coming into play to become a spare man, and it involves making runs and finding space.

These drills employ and refine many of the tactics mentioned above.

Drill One: Using the Keeper

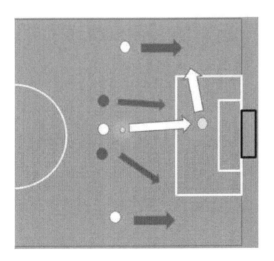

- 4 v 2.

- The player in possession passes to the keeper. Note: work on a particular foot; the keeper needs to be two footed, but he wants a pass he can also hit long first time if necessary.
- The two wide players drop back to receive the pass.
- The two opponents split, one closes the keeper, the other chooses an outfield player to mark.
- Once the ball is played out, the opponents drop off (unless they can win the ball), and the sequence begins again.

Drill Two: Making a run

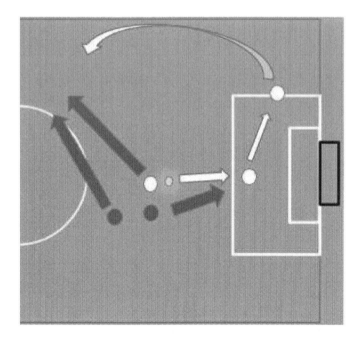

- 3 v 2.
- The ball is laid back with a pass from the striker.
- The striker bends a run into space.
- The recipient of the pass lays a short pass wide.
- A long pass 'in the channel' (i.e., long into space down the wing) is made.
- Opponents start from where indicated, then one tries to pressure the ball, the other marks the attacker making the run

Drill Three: Overlapping Full Backs

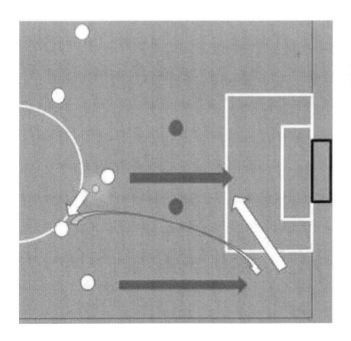

- 5 v 2
- Ball is laid back from one of the advanced midfielders.
- Then it is knocked wide for the full back to run on to.
- The opponents pressure the ball and the nearest players, as they would in a match.
- This creates space for the full backs.
- The two wide defenders alternate making a run forward.
- The side in possession aims to keep possession as long as possible, by restarting the drill from the overlapping position. This helps with practice for transition work.

Drill Four: 5 v 5 + 2

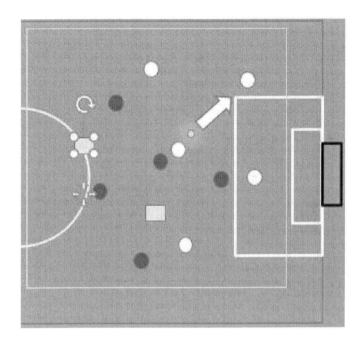

- Another drill involving two spare players.
- There are no goals.
- The aim is to maintain possession for a long as possible.
- Possession switches if an interception is made, or the ball goes out of play.
- The spare players are always on the side of the team in possession.
- The coach looks for movement, good control and a strong, open body position when receiving the ball.

Development

The drill can be made more challenging by reducing the space in which the team plays, or by introducing rules such as two touches maximum or one touch passing.

Drill Five: Full Game

The final drill in this book encompasses all of the exercises and techniques we have covered.

- It is a full sided game.
- Normal rules apply.
- It should be a match situation. The coach or coaches ensure that every player knows their role.
- They ensure that each player has two to three targets to help to improve their own play. They could be tactical, such as telling a wing back to concentrate more on getting forward; they could be technical such as ensuring a striker has his or her body and arms correctly positioned when receiving the ball with back to goal. (Body mass behind, shoulder leading from direction of play, low centre of gravity to withstand physical pressure form behind). Targets could apply to the whole team, or a large group of players, such as the importance of communication.

- Particularly good individual or team play, and particularly weak collective work should result in the game being stopped as soon as appropriate, and the point emphasised. Don't stop the game to pick on an individual negatively; that should be done in private later.
- Remember, even at the highest levels, playing sport should be about enjoyment before anything else.

Final Words

This book of drills and tips will help any individual player or team to improve. The very best coaches, and the players with the most potential, go a step even further.

They are the ones who take the standard types of drill covered in this book, and adapt them to meet the needs of their own sides, or their own individual requirements. So, do look at these drills and see how they can best address those skill and technical shortfalls most apparent in your charges.

Use them as starting points, and make the subtle changes that make them bespoke for your teams' needs; even better, get your players to adapt them themselves, perhaps identifying how a team drill can even more closely focus on a weakness to help the side improve.

Most of all, remember that soccer is about enjoyment, about improving your individual and team skills in the context of a simple, popular sport.

Once the fun stops, so does the point of the game. That, above all, is the key message to every coach, every player and, indeed, every fan of this 'beautiful game.'

Made in the USA
Monee, IL
11 January 2020